Bad Dreams Are Not Allowed!

Written By:
PASHA PERNELL

Illustrated By:
STEVE GREEN

All praises to YHWH because all things are possible through Him....I thank Him...

To my best friend and husband of 8 years, Babe....Thank you for teaching me to be fearless in my dream...I love u..

For my four princesses, Timmi, Jess, Tati, and ChaiYah, your love re-raised me and renews me everyday.....I love you...

The Pastor, The Writer, The World Changer

ISBN-13: 978-0615826998 (Pasha/Pernell)
ISBN: 0615826997

Email: pashapernell@yahoo.com
Website: www.BetHaShemYHWH.com

Printed in the U.S.A.

"Mommy can you put my dreams
on time-out for being so bad?"

It was a sunny morning when Mommy went to
Tatiana's bedroom to wake her up.
As Mommy opened the door, she smiled
at Tatiana and said, "Good morning, Tatiana.
It's time to get up so you can go to school."

Tatiana opened her eyes to see her Mommy.
Then Mommy asked Tatiana,
"Are you ready to explore this beautiful day?"

"Good morning, Mommy. Yes, I guess so,"
Tatiana said with a cloudy face.

Mommy was concerned and wanted to learn more
about this puzzled look, so she asked,
"What wrong, sweet? Your facial forecast tells me
there is a 'not so happy day' trying to look out from
behind that beautiful sun on your face this morning."

"Mommy, my dreams keep misbehaving!"
Tatiana shouted. "Can you put them on time-out?"

Mommy didn't understand what Tatiana was telling her
and asked, "Misbehaving? How are they misbehaving?
Please tell me more."

"Mommy, I keep having bad dreams, and they need a time-out!
Can you put my dreams on time-out for being so bad?"
Tatiana wondered.

"Well, Tatiana, I can tell you how we can make
those dreams of yours behave,"
Mommy said, giving Tatiana hope.

First, you'll start by eating a healthy breakfast,
because **bad dreams are afraid of kids who eat breakfast.**
Breakfast will allow you to power boost your day."

"Really, Mommy?" Tatiana asked with excitement.

"Really!" Mommy assured her.

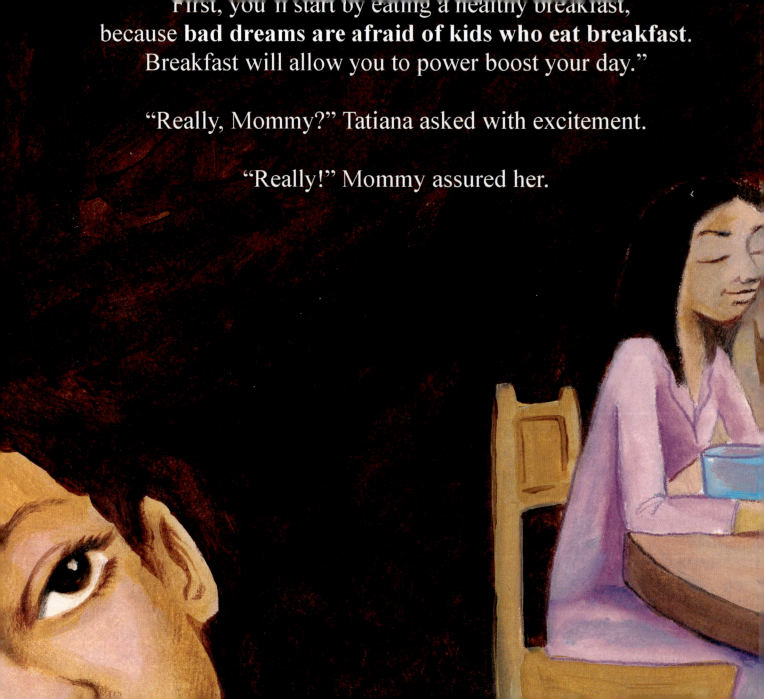

"Next, you'll go to school and learn something new today. You see, **bad dreams are afraid of kids who learn new things.**"

"Okay, Mommy," Tatiana said.

Tatiana sang to herself, "Today, I'm going to learn new things and those bad dreams are going to be afraid."

"Be sure to always do your homework."

"Bad dreams are afraid of kids who do their homework,
because those kids are way smarter than any bad dream."

"I'll do my homework, Mommy," Tatiana replied.

"What else, Mommy, what else?"
Tatiana asked with joy.

"There is another power boost for you at dinnertime.
You'll eat your vegetables for super powers.
Can you guess why?"

"Yes, Mommy!" Tatiana added with a big smile.
**"Bad dreams are afraid of kids who eat their
vegetables to get super powers."**

Mommy chuckled. "Absolutely, sweet. After dinner, we'll get you ready to kick some bubbles at bath time, because **bad dreams are also afraid of those huge bubbles that pop dirt off of your body!**"

"I love bath time, Mommy! I can't wait!" Tatiana yelled.

"Tatiana, you also must always remember to brush your teeth, because **bad dreams are afraid of pretty smiles like yours.**"

Tatiana smiled brightly for practice.

"Lastly, Mommy will tuck you in, and we'll say our prayers for happy thoughts. **Bad dreams are afraid of happy thoughts,** Tatiana."

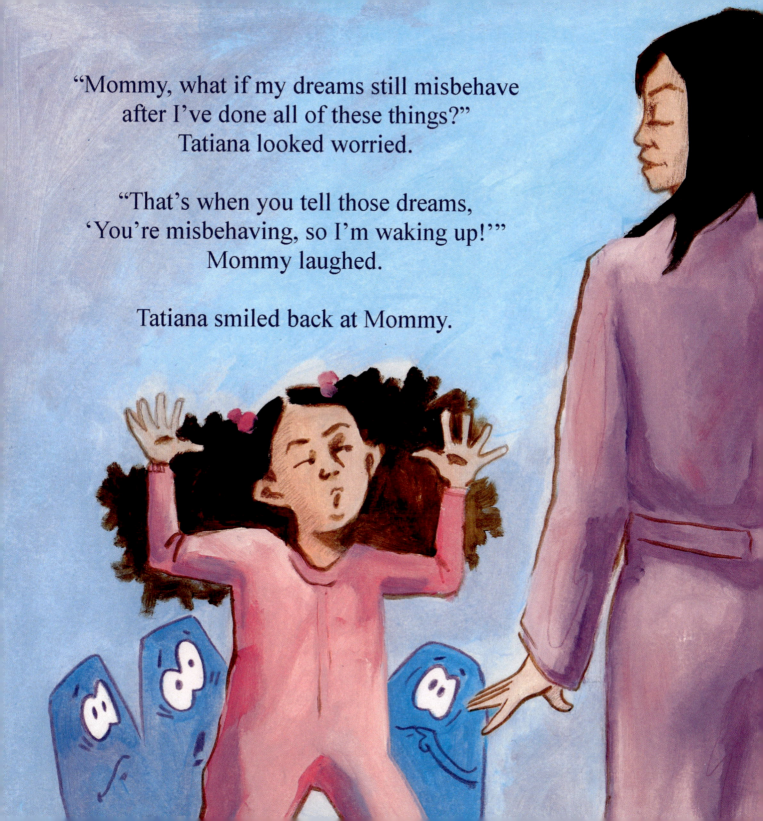

"Mommy, what if my dreams still misbehave
after I've done all of these things?"
Tatiana looked worried.

"That's when you tell those dreams,
'You're misbehaving, so I'm waking up!'"
Mommy laughed.

Tatiana smiled back at Mommy.

Tatiana laughed, too. She felt so much better.
"Thanks, Mommy. I'm ready to explore my day to
scare those bad dreams away!
I love you, Mommy," Tatiana said.

Mommy smiled. "I love you, too, Tatiana."

THE END.

Meet Tatiana!

When my 3-year-old, Tatiana Inez began having nightmares, I felt helpless. I was heartbroken because there was nothing I could do, or so I thought. I would watch her sleep at night, ready to comfort her as soon as she appeared frightened or uneasy.

Then, one night, it hit me! I am her mommy, and I have the power to protect her! Hence, *Bad Dreams Are Not Allowed* came about. Here, Tatiana is encouraged to take control of her nights by practicing healthy habits during the day. This book will encourage your child to face potential problems and brainstorm solutions instead of fearing them.

I hope you enjoy our story and have fun exploring the journey to a great night, just as Tatiana did!

about the author...

Pasha Pernell has always loved to write. From the time she learned the art of storytelling, she immersed herself in the craft.

As an author of short stories, songs, poetry, and rap, she draws upon intimate experiences to captivate the audience in compelling and memorable ways.

Whether playful or functional her prose is refreshingly authentic and engages the young and old alike. Her hope is to add colorful, spirited works to the literary landscape and endear readers the world over.

Pasha is married to Bishop Pernell, her best friend of 8 years. Together they have four beautiful daughters, Timmi Chris 7, Jessica Ann 6, Tatiana Inez 4, and ChaiYah Elite Merlene, 20 months.

Pasha serves as an assistant pastor at Bet HaShem YHWH Worldwide Ministries where she strives to encourage the greatness within each heart. It is her passion and pleasure to uplift souls and help them achieve life success. Her labor is one of love.

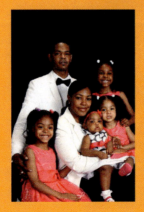

about the illustrator...

Steve Green is an accomplished artist, illustrator and graphic designer who lives and works in the City of Newark, New Jersey. At the age of fourteen years old, Steve envisioned art as his lifelong profession. He began painting and airbrushing shirts and jackets for friends, and discovered that his skills could prove lucrative. He grew as an artist and later attended the Art Institute of Philadelphia earning a degree in Advertising and Graphic Design.

In 1997 he met Bishop Pernell and found his ultimate calling and was ordained a leader in the fivefold ministry under Bet HaShem YHWH Worldwide Ministries. This turning point in life made him determined to use his artistic talents to spread the message of the gospel.

Steve is the owner of Blackbird Artist&Design Studio in Newark, New Jersey where he resides, creating fine and commercial art for both private and public collectors. His work has appeared in a range of galleries and showings, including the Barat Foundation, New Jersey School of Architecture, the Coffee Cave, and City Without Walls Gallery.

Due to his artistic excellence and passion for urban renewal, he has been commissioned to execute large scale murals throughout Greater Essex County, including the B.R.I.C.K. Avon Academy and Firehouse Mural Commission in Newark. Not only does he see art as a way to revitalize the soul, but also a way to re-imagine our communal living space, and stimulate creativity and pride within all citizens.

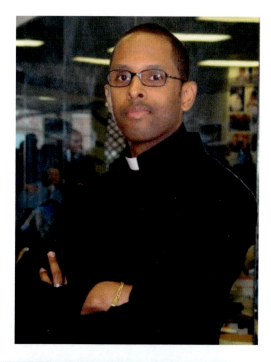

Made in the USA
Middletown, DE
10 November 2023